To Collect the Flesh

POEMS BY
Greg Hewett

Minnesota Voices Project Number 73

New Rivers Press 1996

New Rivers Press is a non-profit literary press dedicated to publishing the very best emerging writers in our region, nation, and world.

The publication of *To Collect the Flesh* has been made possible by generous grants from the Jerome Foundation, the Metropolitan Regional Arts Council (from an appropriation by the Minnesota Legislature), the National Endowment for the Arts, the North Dakota Council on the Arts, the South Dakota Arts Council, Target Stores, Dayton's and Mervyn's by the Dayton Hudson Foundation, and the James R. Thorpe Foundation.

Additional support has been provided by the Elmer L. and Eleanor J. Andersen Foundation, the Beim Foundation, Bush Foundation, General Mills Foundation, Liberty State Bank, the McKnight Foundation, the Minnesota State Arts Board (through an appropriation by the Minnesota Legislature), the Star Tribune/Cowles Media Company, the Tennant Company Foundation, and the contributing members of New Rivers Press. New Rivers is a member agency of United Arts.

To Collect the Flesh has been manufactured in Canada for New Rivers Press, 420 North 5th Street, Minneapolis, MN 55401. First Edition.

To Collect the Flesh

For Tony Hainault,
who has kept me collected,
and in memory of my father,
Jack Hewett.

Acknowledgments

The following poems have appeared in these publications: "The Corinthians Reply" and "Cruising at 30,000 Feet" in *Anti-Dog;* "Man Talk," "Monument," and "Mr. Okamoto's Dream" in *The Hamline Review;* "Father Installs Shower" in *Pacific Review;* "SAID" in *Art and Understanding;* "Garbo Behind Black Screen" in *Interim;* "So to Speak As They Say" in *5 A.M.;* "The Kimono-maker Contemplates Ice" and "Aquarium" in *Saint Andrews Review;* "Waterhouse" and "The Ugly Swan" in *The Little Magazine;* "Ode to a Penis" in *The James White Review;* "Walking Alone in Ørsteds Park" in *The Body Politic;* "George Washington, Lover" in *The Wormwood Review;* "Finlandia" in *Image;* "A Frog from Bashō in *Scriveners Rampant.*

Table of Contents

I Unstrung

TARZAN IS DEAD

The radio announces
Tarzan is dead.

The next item I can see:
a blizzard

smothers the dark firs
out my window.

As a boy with measles
evergreens became ghosts

with the snow and my fever
poured from the TV

jungle-movie
Tarzan Finds a Son.

All I desired
was for delirium to last

so I could be a son
who was his father's

companion forever
living high in the trees

facing leopards bravely
swimming under falls.

With a stomp of galoshes
on porch-boards

my father entered shaking
snow from his coat.

Flakes fell like feathers
from a manly eagle-

like angel descended
from Kilimanjaro.

His Arctic hands enclosed
my face and still hold

as I go to my own porch
far from his and dip my hands

in snow colder than tropical
pools. Heat and fever

hold no pleasure for Tarzan
is dead, he died

on his veranda
in Acapulco

where under golfing slacks
medics discovered a loincloth

and neighbors complained
about jungle-calls at 3 A.M.

The phone rings: my father
who is living

calling long-distance
calling over the Atlantic

calling through a veil
of snow to tell me:

Tarzan is dead.

FATHER INSTALLS SHOWER, CA. 1962

And then there was rain
and he was pleased

He laughed thunder
and it echoed off cold

walls He protected
my upturned face

with shoulders broad
as a tortoise

and his whiskered kiss
blessed and his flesh

hung promising
as a gourd in the desert

that never burst
or ran or trickled

in my mouth
Like the rain

all illusion
not a word

more like a note
from an unstrung lyre

a note with no lyric
fixing it to earth
(this-means-that)

a long note humming
over deserted

Atlantis
through my bowels

these years
Since then

I have seen him only
on the other side

of thick glass
etched with waves

and sea-shells
and sea-horses

and the water won't stop
and drowning I seek

the tortoise on whose back
the world rides

on whose shell
the music is strung

MANTALK

1.

I was born when you were 29
the year of your birth and now

                    in '87 the numbers add up:
                    I am 29 and you are dead at 58

                    the year of my birth.
                    A riddle these numbers neat

and predictable as death.
But numerology is no science

I want real numbers.
The physical fact

                    is father

I am disintegrating.
I figure my half-life

is up: alpha-beta-gamma
a fraternity excited

                    to leave in search
                    of your omega yet

there is no beginning or end
to the infinite traces of you.

We share the same matter
scrambled though hardly

arbitrary
(that's genetics).

Light years away
do we appear

29, 58, 87, all the years
simultaneously

twins when time becomes
superfluous?

2.

The one place you never were
and wanted to go

are you there now?
Are you floating up fjords

on a postal ship?
I can just see it

the means unpretentious
the scenery sublime.

This has something to do
with baseball and the peace

you found in its numbers
and geometry made imperfect

by men.

3.

I have never
held a grudge

                              or single black thought
                              against you

or your new ghost
the way children

                              of the same sex
                              are supposed to.

But I, your honey, sweetheart
darling, want to talk

anyway, to hear this way
you usually talked

                              to me
                              a language familiar

to lovers
men sometimes

didn't understand.
We were so ignorant

                              of the language of men.

GEORGE WASHINGTON, LOVER

I always preferred the quiet life
                                not here

in the Great Beyond, but above
                                in the Blue

Ridge Mountains hunting,
fishing, hiking with my friend
                                and brother, Lawrence.

And certainly not *there*
below, along the banks of the miasmic Potomac.

No, not there where I never delivered
                                any of those words

not even those noble
                fading words the painting of my Farewell
                would have you believe I uttered.

All P.R. for my apotheosis.
I didn't even write my Farewell.
Hamilton did

as I watched a cloud
of white hair, an old woman
                        undone, a good wife
                        hurrying through the cherry orchard

looking frantically for the one
who had left her.
                She might have been Martha or maybe not . . .

If I could just speak
                to Alexander, have him

explain
I'm just a man.
            At least for a while

our voices
were one, or
rather
      I was the silence
      between his words

a brooding silence.
I brooded

over the lie beyond
the cherry tree, the lie
          of his love
          which wasn't love at all
                but a sign

of the times: no *eros*
but love only
as a means
        to establish a state
        as if a representative body could satisfy.

I don't know which of us was the bigger
                whore
                and though the tower was built
                in my name he was the one
                who babbled on about power.

To remember that one voice
I have to go to the beginning.
Alexander's beginning, which seems more
than coincidental with my brother Lawrence's end.

Alexander the ambition
                    and sin of Hellas in a word.

Alexander born under
                    the only volcano in Barbados.

A drunken Scotsman took his French mother
in a room one fine Caribbean noon

a room of shadows,
a filthy room, the shadow and filth

of my desire
a disease never attached
                    to Lawrence, the real
                    Virginia blue blood, the man I nursed
                    three years before Alexander's birth

as he lay dying
                under a canopy
                in the trade-wind
                in the volcanic sand
                of that archipelago
                where Alexander would be spawned
                that land so far from fecund

Virginia, land
                of the Virgin Queen.

Even then I knew
somewhere in my witchy self
knew I was nourishing
                    desire

around Lawrence's absence, a desire

> that would bring about
> a miraculous birth
> an emperor
> a conqueror
> an Alexander
> something queer
> to America.

You see I wanted my brother, the hero

> of the French and Indian
> War, to be my lover.

In Lawrence's delirium I'd talk
as a lover talks

> and interpret his moan as reply.

Then I'd turn to the surf
to rinse the linens

> of sweat and think

pensive, doubtful thoughts
as if we'd just made love.

I clearly know Lawrence
would have made something

> of our country, something

not all illusion.
Something real.

> He had the words
> and the silence
> and they were one.
> The impossible tongue.

He would never have stood
in this empirical empire

where objects are boldly contoured
objects, nothing more, and no more ideas

but in things
           that can be seen through
           telescope and microscope.

Had he not died
I would have stayed
           in his shadow
           and been happy.

The length of my own shadow
isn't much, the outline indefinite

which made it easy
for Alexander to shadow me
           make my moves like voodoo.

When I first saw Alexander
charging abouta battlefield
           outside New York, I knew

he was charmed and I was
           the charm.

I also knew he wouldn't die
in battle, but ridiculously
           when his luck ran out
           after he ran from me.

For the Revolution our romance thrived.
                  Ruggedly

under horse-blankets
           French-style
           he put his half-French tongue

14

in my mouth
after which I never spoke

        a word
        of my own

especially not when he told me to order

            the buggers in the regiment
            put before the firing-squad
            to take the heat for us.

Hamilton dominated

        and I gave in
        to him and gave up

power for what I thought

        was love.
        The problem was my love

still didn't make
his birth
      right.

Who would listen to
a dark illegitimate boy
from Barbados
raised by a Jew?

        So he married Schuyler-New York-Nobility
        I introduced him to

and left me alone

        with widow Martha.
        I married the dowry
        to be given my brother.

Even when he no longer pretended

        to love me
        I did as he willed.

When I said New York
would be the Seat of Empire
I meant it as a figure of speech.
                        No poet, he took me
                        at face value, wanting all roads
                        leading to New York.

He couldn't have done it without me.
I placed the great weight of my silence
                        behind my love
                        and never sought revenge.

I consented to this country
as you know it
for love
        of a man
        and nothing
                    more

nothing less.
In the beginning
            was love . . .

He made me No Man's Man
a No Man's Land on the Potomac.
                        But I'm a person
                        not just a place.

How could he establish a void
                    in my heart?
                    D.C.'s like love
                    without a heart.

16

L'Enfant's great Parisian arteries
suggest flux, blood.
>But all the granite and marble
monuments, the documents
harden there like cholesterol
something we didn't worry about
or even know about then.

Heart-attack and then
>Stasis came to these States.

If only we could make revolutions
make love

again
return to the pure
idea which is only pure

in the crude
vagueness of its expression:
>*I love you.*

Somewhere between those warm
West Indian sands
>and the frozen
blankets at Valley Forge

all was realized—
I spoke my own words:

I love you Alexander—
and all was lost.

He said nothing
but nothing
>remembered is lost.

Maybe there is only silence
like a pure light

        and the moment
        anything becomes
        a shadowed thing and speaks
        it dies. History is dying.

He lives
        only in my desire and the mind
        of some scholars

while I live
        in your collective desire

buried by wig and velvet
coat-tails and breeches.

As I speak now
        antlers gone from my mouth
        I flabbergast your books.

Love is dying too.
And I don't mean declining
but a series
of deadly utterances.
        Deaths.

Battle to battle
        we lived, loved
            onward!
Afterwards all was dead
as the Constitution
as inaugurals.
        Already I could feel
        my death-mask cast
        my profile minted.

I frightened Alexander
                    to death

with my declaration
                    of love.
                    I wounded
                                    his masculinity.

With my queer foresight
                    I knew he was dead
                    when I left Washington.

Two widows
Martha and I
                    retired to Mount Vernon.

Without my silence only words
small words, mean words, filled the capital.

Infighting
                    they say, but it is no fighting
                    just a cowardly violence of minds.

Alexander didn't know
what he was saying.
                    He thought he could keep on speaking
                    for me and found himself
                    with no mouthpiece.

Siding with his old enemy Jefferson
                                    he wound up dead

at the hands of Burr
above the bluff
on the marshy plain
of Weehawken.

(When he expired did he think of me already in heaven?)

Where's the bespectacled doctor?
The white-bearded nurse?
                              This is an emergency!
                              I need words!

No sand, no snow, a place
                    of poetry

this New Jersey
now in the shadows
                    of billboards, refineries
                    structures you don't see

in Washington, D.C.
But I tell you the obelisk
and all the other Olympian
                              memorials sheathed in marble
                              are the same as this.

A pimp pulls up
hassles his trade.
An old woman,

white hair, I almost recognize,
picks for scraps.
                    I can talk here
                    tell the truth in her
                              presence.

Even all the cherry trees in bloom
could not white this mistake out

this United States
          of Alexander!

20

We should have left
for the wilderness

and surveyed
as I once did
                with Lawrence.

That is all I really wanted:
                        to know
                        the lay
                                of the land.

We never would have made maps
                            or built an empire and love

would have made
                our words
                honest
                        as the surveyor's level.

But in this place good words are
                            forgotten

replaced by curses:
                *Fuck you
                Alexander!*

And I finally recognize
                the old woman.

She has been scorned, abandoned

breathes her own poison
                        words

because her life has become
                        a lie

because all she has worked for
                              and loved
                              has left.

Yes, she swears
at the world
then leaves
                   dissolving
                   in benzedrine dreams.

Drugged, stumbling
                          with green backs

of Alexander and me
                         our faces crumpled
                         in her house-dress.

she heads to the dirty river
smeared with chemicals.
                              I am that good wife.

II Myth

THE UGLY SWAN

As you know, my feathers whitened
                    neck arced and wings grew seraph-sized.

When I hoisted them to the breeze
                    looking like one of those boats

entering the tunnel of love you probably thought
                    I had smooth sailing
                    ever after.

Sure I was glad to be rid of those
                    ridiculing ducks
                    iridescent heads

smoldering
                    green as hell
                    green with envy

as I, casual as a serpent
                    turned back
                    to look
                    just once.

                    But that was only the beginning.
                    The story was always the same.

No Whistler or Whooper would have one
                    black, no
                    not swan, but sheep

while Trumpeters blasted
                    me for being mute
                    because Mute

Swans they swore
                    would sing only sorrow
                    the Biggest Blues
                    a Swan Song.

They didn't say it
              but I could tell

the Mutes thought I was one of those
who turned human
              from time to time.

But even with a mythic flock
                        it's a myth:
                        birds of a feather don't.

While others turned into Zeus
                        Lohengrin the swan knight
                        and princess
                        ballerina, I came ashore

not in any opera or ballet corps
                        but in a litter-

filled public park, a sewer
                        not Swan Lake.

I had relations
              with those who have

no other
        strangers all, they left me

at dawn as I
          left them, knowing

what I tell you:
              we are all cygnets

in nests of ducklings
                   so what's the difference?

MUSICAL CHAIRS

you took my chair and I don't mind
you took my head-of-the-table-
daddy-ordering-grace-and-demanding-
mashed-potatoes-chair and I don't care
you took my captain's chair and that was perfect
what with Pinkerton the sailor
and a Butterfly glorious as Victoria
des Los Angeles singing in the background
because Japan's a country without chairs
and because I was perhaps wondering
who resembled the *geisha*
and who was going to sail
and wasn't it an evening lush as Puccini
extraordinary as opera
you took my chair and I was glad
someone was in the driver's seat so no one got taken
for a ride no wreck no *seppuku*
verismo without the expected tragedy
though we had the premise
in fact the whole score written
and underscored by ominous
tubas and kettle drums humorous to us as taboos
you took my chair and I don't mind
and no well maybe I had something in mind
and maybe you did too when we stood
and said good-night and didn't and then did
what maybe we had in mind (seated however deeply)
you took no chair when the music stopped
and I don't care don't mind the game made no sense
what with two chairs for two the bed held more
possibilities for instance the impossible.

SO TO SPEAK AS THEY SAY

Not that I'd been thinking about you or anything
like that but maybe hoping somewhere
in what's called the back of the mind
we'd run or is it bump
into each other like as they say
two ships in the night or do they
just pass anyway there
you were faraway and it was
like a dream except this great puddle
of water and oil which are never supposed to mix
this pool in the parking-lot came
between us and it had rainbows
and neither of us wanted
to get our feet wet so to speak
we talked across this hardly
romantic abyss like perfect
no like imperfect as the case may be strangers

A FROG FROM BASHŌ

Monsoons have filled
the ricefields.

Mosquitoes rise
filaments

sewing the night.
Minute

electronic noise.
Disquiet.

A sweatshop
not bedroom.

Sleepless
and robbed

of blood
we sweat

watch our dreams
ripped off

like limp sheets.
Don't touch me

you protest.
I strike

the *futon* and think
how other summers

we worked so well
together

allowed sweat
to oil

our parts
and in the morning

we'd scratch bites
make love

again and doze
till noon.

To be
reincarnated

as a frog
from Bashō!

My mouth
would tear

these seams
from the air

cool breeze
would shuttle through

and my swelling
throat would lull

you to sleep
with a song

weaving me
anew

in your malarial
dreams.

JET-LOVE

Everything you have asked is done: my keys
are on the Korean chest; the landlord
has taken my name from the lease; I leave
Osaka in a few hours aboard
a flight you scheduled. In San Francisco
I'll sort the accumulation in storage,
sell the Danish table and curio,
tear photos. Even letters I have courage
to part with. Possession has bought me
only loss, brought me no place. I'll have my own place
by the time you return from Italy.
In New York I'll rent dreams of solace:
all the rooms we've ever shared are on fire
and you call across time zones for me, for fear.

WALKING ALONE IN ØRSTEDS PARK

that place of lovers
we always skirted
following the fence of iron
lilies and breathing the diesel
of the perimeter instead.

At its heart a lake.
On shore greened bronzes
one of two Greeks
wrestling or making love
monumentally.

Buds on branches severely
pruned last fall give
direction. Two women
sprawl on the lawn
in the future

shade, lovers
beside the wrestlers.
Free from pedestal
they bend over
laugh at reflections.

They swim naked
ignoring cold
and regulations
confident their course
won't disturb

this romantic body
designed with
no nameable shape.
The lake, the whole park
is at the mercy of their mirth

their cries in Icelandic
the splashing. The green men writhe
on the surface.
This is no mirror.
This is joy.

FRENCH FORMAL

Don't count me in. Your garden has statues
and specimens enough. Besides, the formal
symmetry goes unrecognized except
at the axis, and only you frequent
the scalloped balcony aligning
the Venus Fountain with the Arch of Mars.
I'm out of line or more precisely
I am he who wanders the garden
ignoring raked pebble paths as I home in
on the blackest shrubs and reddest flowers
trampling the well-planned sunbursts and arabesques
in my pursuit of extremes. Ignorant
of the rare and Latin, I prefer vulgar
lichen, silver and scarlet, scarring
balustrade and urn, blackberry canes
obstructing statuary, strangling hedgerows,
wildflowers of any kind. You have to learn
these modern times, when the ground erupts
with automatic sprinklers. Baroque plans
are long over, and you're no minotaur.
This boxwood maze holds no one intent
on escape. I'll chase the arbitrary
shadows of cloud, step way out of bounds.
If you would admit my undrafted line
you could follow. From the forest
your careful grounds are seen only
as interruption, dangerous
as an open field incised by a hunter's sights.

THE CORINTHIANS REPLY

You speak in jive of fools and the devil.
You're just static a bad tune muzak with this love.
If you had the gift of mockery
enough smarts to know you're gonna get burned
you wouldn't have love you'd have something.
If you gave away all you had and used your body
to earn and didn't have love you'd gain something.
Love is insatiable and hopeless
it rejoices in deceit not in truth.
Love obscures all things believes in nothing
corrupts all things fucks up all things.
Love has evil in mind.
Love always ends   as for secrets
they'll be revealed   as for tongues
they'll talk   as for pride   it will leave.
Pride and respect are perfect
but when the imperfect comes the perfect will pass away.
When we were in love we spoke crazy
we thought and understood crazy
but when we came to we gave up
crazy things and began to see
through a shot glass clearly. Face it.
Now you know in your heart   later you won't know at all
fractions in you of desire lust   and sex
and of these great three   the greatest is sex.
Sex is the greatest.

GARBO BEHIND BLACK SCREEN

By myself, my face will do things
I cannot do with it otherwise . . .

1.

Garbo's apartment in New York
contains nothing

black-and-white.
What with all her movies

she thought
black-and white

contains no warmth.
Red-gold morocco-

bound volumes
light the walls

like fire
and she loved Heine best

as much as Hollywood
Squares, Ming jars

green porcelain
parrots and Louis XV furniture.

Impressionists
especially

Renoirs
with all those colors

she hid behind drapes
as if she knew

the punishment
for too much beauty.

His "Confidence"
("The Secret," in English)

a woman whispering
in the ear

of a man, only special
guests could see.

In Madame de Pompadour's chair
only a snowman

plastic, inflated
could sit.

How cold?
How funny?

2.

In the age of technicolor
alone in her *chambre*

with little light intruding
through the louvers

she practiced
expressions discrete

as an alphabet
complete as a lexicon.

Ill-illumined
yet perfect

as any star
under lights

brilliant
as film on fire

a performance all
for the Mediterranean air.

There was never an audience
and she would curse

the shadows out the window
I can say you never existed . . .

3.

As a girl in her
first job

silent
as a movie

she mimed
the ugly

mugs of men
she lathered

mastering the art
of masculinity.

All she masked
she remembered

saved for some future
speech, a manly Anna

Christie crying, *Ah!*
Whadduz it mattah?

Or when their leers disappeared
nervous under her razor

inside she laughed endlessly
like Ninotchka would years later.

4.

For close-ups Garbo
demanded purdah

black screens assembled
around her and no visitors'

eyes only the camera.
Not for shame or

embarrassment.
Metamorphosis.

From what she called
just a woman making faces

5.

to perfect myth
an obsidian

Aztec butterfly
in a desert

of absolute white.
Meaning gravitates

to those black wings
adds no weight.

She robs the air
of substance

with her flight.
We never saw her

tracing her legend
the celluloid Elgin marbles.

6.

Faced with a Napoleonic
press-corps

using her as his army used
the place of virgins

the Parthenon
as an arsenal

and ready to blow
her top, she inscribed

the war of words
I choose as a weapon

complete silence.
Defeated

we try to imagine what
the Sphinx looks like

undamaged, nose replaced
features unworn

by sand and wind or what
she would say beyond

I want to be
(left) (let) alone.

AQUARIUM

Behind glass we're learning
not to fear the sea.
Without waves

little resemblance
to the body
crossed for centuries

though perhaps truer
from this fish perspective.
Below the surface

complex volume:
a coral garden
clouds with sand

as a stingray
ascends.
We don't know such space.

How do we learn
to descend a tree
of kelp without aqualung

to breathe the stream?
Complete strangeness
erases

a tribal memory
of lungs
filling with water

as our fingers release
splintered flotsam
the very same wood

of houses voyaged
too far from
in boats too like houses.

Truth is no one goes
far enough.
With no Atlantis

We're not ourselves
but become
no one

specific creature.
The starfish
prying an oyster

emptying it
except for the pearl.
The anemone at ease

as an angel.
The clam burning
with a zealot's faith

with slow acid
through stone to mate
in a self-made tomb.

But we should leave
these lessons
in bathos and suspend

the desire
to turn all things human.
At last prepared

we arc toward the far blur
of sun in a school
languid as so much

confetti released.
The surface boils
with foil bodies

dorsal fins slice
the true air and we dive
in earnest.

YOUNG FLORENTINE SCULPTOR

She wants to carve
Medusa's face
beautiful so beautiful
and sexual
it will mirror all
desire lost
in the shadowy
Gorgon cave
of manners
centuries of manners.

When she told her father
she was lesbian
he cried

"We might have expected
it from another
not so *bella* girl
you know the type
who doesn't care
what she looks like
the kind who wouldn't
get a boy
if she tried
the kind who won't
bleach shave
or electrolysize
her whiskers
when she becomes
a woman.
But you
my daughter are
all glossy
pony-tail
girl-allure

under that over
-sized sweater.
All my friends
whistle and call
when you glide by
on your Vespa."

She said, "Papa,
I am more
like a boy
the way boys can be
more like girls
than girls sometimes
if you really look."

And he threw up
his arms and yelled
she was no daughter
of his
and she agreed.

She curses
whenever she passes
Cellini's monument
to Perseus murderer
of Medusa and she thinks
she will outdo him, undo him.

She cannot tell
what her statue
will look like other
than to say it will be
exactly what she sees

when on certain
late nights or early
mornings, half-conscious

she catches her reflection
and is drawn
to her own
body. It
won't be marble
or any known material
won't be
naturalistic
in a usual sense.

Features
neither female nor
male but no
hermaphrodite.

When she unveils
the new Medusa
right there
in the Piazza
della Signoria
the body of the other
will rise from Perseus' feet
take her head from his hand
place it back
on her own shoulders
leaving him
to pose
with a fistful
of serpents
as she joins
her sister
on a pedestal
no man built.

MR. OKAMOTO'S DREAM

This local to Kyoto shakes
stops at many stations covered
with dust and too much light
from neighboring *pachinko* parlors.
Small salaries shrink
on their way home from Osaka.

I have bigger dreams . . .
Beyond the fence lies
a separate airport-sleek station.
Shinkansen passes through
on other rails
like, as they say in English, a bullet,

without jerking or effort
heading with swollen speed
for unfamiliar
destinations, an ancient
on-sen, a hot-spring,
with casino perhaps.

I envision a peculiar
elegance: Japanese
technology arriving
at a Victorian
casino, calcium-white
beside a cold lake,

a spectacular place where
one could take or leave
a fortune if one could
interpret the subtle
clucking of the oracle,
the roulette wheel.

There I would become
the tuxedoed hero
under chandeliers.
I would certainly reserve
a reclining seat home
or be rowed by grateful men

across the perfect lake
at the very edge of dawn
to a private car
in the antiquated
steam train and then ride
down the wilder shore.

But the bullet-train passes through
leaving a trail of sparks
in the stone-colored sky
like violets suddenly
discarded by diva or contessa
when you eventually lose.

There is I believe
more honor in such loss.
Perhaps just today
I will stop and play at Mama-san's
MONACO or Hiroshi's VEGAS
the silly pin-ball game and win

in the neon of their famous names
that are not those places,
win the fare to the place by the lake
that needs no sign, the place
where you simply know
when you have arrived.

THE KIMONO-MAKER CONTEMPLATES ICE

1.

One dawn ice appears
thin and startling
on the surface of the bath.

Scarlet leaves fallen
in the *koi* pond
will be spared the fire

though there is life in ice
killing color slowly.
Spring will find brown scraps

the hue of elders'
kimonos turning
in iceless currents.

2.

When ice remains
thick yet half-melted
it is apparent

there are more
than four seasons
of the sun.

I refuse
red maple as emblem
of autumn

or parabolic
drifts and obvious
geometry

of snowflakes
as a sign
of winter.

Under the celadon pond
dead lotus
leaves like beaten gold

disks pulse
in the sun
vines like twisted wire

ancient jewelry
suspended around
no remains.

This scene
I will weave
into a bridal

kimono
leaving a new bride
to define the body

of water
between two states
to suggest

the Heian princess
such a necklace
once encircled

the girl
who the story says
drowned herself

on her wedding day
to spare her husband
rumors that followed her beauty.

3.

In this age
I lament we adventure
beyond our islands.

Like Europeans
we wrestle with the Arctic
just to plant patches

of national color
on infinite
white.

We forget we come
from a country
where the aim of archery

is not the target
to even look at a bullseye
vanity.

In such a case
90° north looms less
important than comprehending

a land with no earth
where *night* and *day*
name seasons

where all other
places stand
away.

An explorer resists
the cold
with tropical images

trusts mylar too much
never learns
the element.

Such a man will not
declare death
evident

will presume survival
on the ice
will intend to assemble

the nylon flag
an official gave him
folded deep in his pack.

4.

Our traditional color
of mourning
is white:

the ceiling
walls, floor, we cover
with white cloth

woven so fine
the weave is
invisible.

The funeral house
is like the mind
when thoughts surrender

to a peaceful death
the explorer
might never experience

but a monk
in meditation
on a mountain

ignorant
of coming
snows

in his ragged
summer kimono
he knows.

III Figures

AMBER IS FOR CAUTION

(Christmas 1990)

Eyes of pigeons shine as they fly
into the coming storm.
Swaying dangerously like a lost ship

at the empty intersection
a traffic light moves
between green and red.

That pause lengthens and you drive through
as though time were resin.
Seems anachronistic

to recollect collecting amber
alone on a far northern shore
in this urgent time, this climate.

Definitely Romantic as the Baltic
swelling in winter: ships split on icebergs,
abysses, the Sublime, etcetera.

Remember holding amber
to icy light and seeing
two armored insects suspended

eons ago, like warring kings.
Pollen glittered. Trees, a whole forest
of firs in a drop, and they were on fire,

a deep red shadow on the sun.
Scratches like strokes of axes
and suddenly trees were falling

and sand and dust
were rising, and sunlight
solidifying. Almost atomic,

this clearing for towns
before the Amber Road connected
Copenhagen, Pomerania,

Prague, Budapest, Istanbul,
all the way to Baghdad,
before these places existed

before amber or oil
or traffic and traffic lights
or you or I in traffic.

Almost atomic

how these civilizations
turned to sand.
Maybe not so

ridiculous to recollect
collecting amber, what with Iraq
and Arabia about to glow

in the desert fierce
as the brooch of a Viking
warrior big as Orion, ready to explode

with that kind of fission
discovered in stars.
Who can thank god

at the apex
of the *Cathedra Petri*
in the shape of a dove

supposedly ascending
but more like flapping
in a spider's web of amber

light made of lead and glass?
The spirit can not move.
Petrified.

The fathers remain
in the driver's seat,
fuel is low.

AT MANTEGNA'S PAINTING OF ST. SEBASTIAN

Of course arrows pierce his torso
and from his forehead

        the critical one protrudes

My eyes hurt: a shadowless noon

            marks the suffering
            makes me see

I stand outside the frame
of any holiness

      with the archers
      who do not cry

as they unstring their bows
who have no shame for killing

          desire that ribbons
          of blood can only adorn

who have bound the strength

          of his faith his flesh
          to a ruined arch

At his bare feet the sandalled feet
of their crumbled emperor

          in the weeds heads
          of their old gods

Look
in a corner of the sky

        the almost invisible

god in a chariot of cloud
veering earthward

        to collect the flesh